Ambergris

First Edition

ISBN: 978-1-963110-21-0

Published by

Pine Row Press

www.pinerow.com

For permissions or inquiries, please contact:

Pine Row Press

Ft Mitchell, KY

contact@pinerow.com

Ambergris

Amy Dryansky

Pine Row Press
Ft Mitchell, KY

For Tovi and Isaac, who helped make this book, and for John,
who is here in these pages, if not in this world.

Even the term ambergris is the result of a misunderstanding.

—*A Brief, Fascinating History of Ambergris*, Hakai Magazine

Contents

III

Ambergris

What I believed in was a flower, symmetrical,
predictable: *cruciform, coronate, campanulate.* A flower
real and imaginary, contained in its own logic.
Try to see it in your mind's eye. Before the petals fade
and drop. Follow the drift of it, river of it, depth,
bottom of it. Fathom that, you and your whale,
your anchor, your quest. What can't be digested made
precious—like ambergris—or the way a mollusk
builds a pearl from irritation and nacre. The strangeness
of that. Like the guy who said a whale swallowed him
by accident. He thought it was over. His existence.
Had time to think it, before the whale in its irritation
at the not-krill in the sieve of its legendary maw
spit the man back out. Spit him out entire. Fabulous,
lustrous story no one believes, intact.

Between

I watch as a spotted cow tenderly licks another cow
beneath an ear shaped like one leaf of a four-leaf clover

in a barnyard shouldered between secondary roads
and a brand-new modular home, where three guys heave-ho

at a cable big around as my arm, trying to get the house
hooked up to a utility pole, and for some reason

they remind me of subjects in a painting, a bucolic pastoral,
or a heroic tableau of some legendary battle's pivotal moment—

planting a flag, hauling in a lifeboat of the half-drowned—
you know, the kind where if anyone's dying, they're doing it

so monumentally it's only an aesthetic, abstracted kind of sad?
I rely on that distance. Anything to keep the brick off my chest.

But I can't stop looking, either, and the cows are spavined,
underfed, the house someone punched the clock hard to buy

is ugly, almost windowless. And the men are stalled. They spit,
look defeated. Then again, maybe I'm wrong, maybe they're just

taking a break. I can't always tell the difference between sad
and sweet; sometimes they taste the same to me. It's a confusion

to which I'm prone, an allegiance, I won't say religion, but
it could be the only way I know how to pray. I keep tasting that ear,

tongue, those muscled backs, sweat and indecision, tenderness,
disappointment. A little bite of each, a redistribution of weight,

a feeling like a door in my chest scraping across its threshold,
and something else, a vibration, maybe a swarm of bees.

Sweet

Sap's flowing,   galvanized
buckets ride the maples, making little factories
lit from within

(factories or bodies)

and because my leg aches again
I'm certain what I've dreaded—a deviation, some key
        linkage in my body's chromosomal chain
        askew—

has finally come to roost
Injured bird, insistent song, my mother's parting shot
from a bed she couldn't leave:
No one gives you a gold star, honey.

Meaning: give up fantasy, sweet distraction
I drink straight from the tap.

Meaning: I haven't called to see if the hawk we found
recovered from its collision with a car.

I'd rather guess

from here, make a better story, but I can't
invent a different ending

for the nine boys killed collecting firewood
in the desert
        from high above
by drones
on a screen, with a joystick

by other boys (almost men)
recruited in video arcades. (Somebody's brainstorm.)

It's a job
(people need to eat)
someone still has to get firewood

and even the man in my town
who fixes birds
handled the injured hawk so casually
it was hard to reconcile.

He didn't promise anything

and there's another man I read about
who's made it his work
          to bring people together
with the people who've hurt them

he doesn't try to get them to forgive
or be forgiven, but they have to look at each other
and listen.

I was afraid to hold the hawk
afraid more than the wing
          might be broken

and I wanted to close my mother's eyes

after she died
but I couldn't
                    I was too late.
Nothing soft was left.

Wasp's Nest

Gray sack, slowly deflating balloon. Where the wasps
have gone to, I haven't a clue. I know nothing

about the world's physicalities, the facts. I make things up,
draw pictures, play a game in my head. The nest fell.

Maybe I hit it with my broom. The other wasps are probably
looking down at me from a canopy of maples

on my walk, tracing invisible dotted lines down the hill
past the red house with a room shaped like a silo

built by a man who's dead. His wife lives there alone,
and she isn't eating well. I keep worrying

I should do something, but I don't. Next to her
there's the guy who's always hosing down his driveway,

raking gravel out of his lawn. If we were in a fire
or on a sinking ship, I wouldn't be the first person he'd save.

But if wasps were chasing me and I banged on his door
he'd open it. I'd stand on the mat

careful not to track in mud and we'd talk
about how terrible an angry wasp can be, and when it was safe

I'd leave. That would be our common ground,
like the wasps and me: no sting, just recognition.

Caution Tape

The world's become inhospitable, ungentle, no room
in the hospital, no safety, just smoke, smoke, more
smoke, then rain, more rain, too much rain, no harbor,
no dock, you can't and if you do, there's no guarantee,
no healing, no respite, no test, no hospice, not even
an easy way to die, no path, no map, no one to ask
or tell but your own exhausted, inhospitable, precarious
self, yourself, your cells that could house the virus
waiting to kill you, not now, but later, or maybe now,
while you're alone in your brick-and-mortar box
of a house, disintegrating box of your body, its permeable
vessels, aerosols, gray tangle of impulses, blown fuses,
outages, downed wires, underwater emergency calls
where they ask where you are, and you can't say
exactly because you're lost, and that road, ma'am,
is closed, ma'am, did you hear me, did you happen
to get the make and model, take down a plate?
No, I didn't get the plate, note a location, just that
you weren't there when I needed you, where
did you go and where do we go, how do we know
where to go when there is no more home, now that
here isn't home, now that here, my body, is nowhere?

(Eve) Talking to Herself (Mother's Day)

You start where you always start, with the body. You like
to get close, imagine body as landscape, yourself supine
among furred hills, muscular plains. Let's be more specific.
You're restless. Let's be direct. You're unreliable.
You shift. You're itching to get back to that leafy spot
where you trampled the grass, *culminated* your heart out,
crossed innocence, that narrow divide. When it comes
to infidelity you're torn. You're tempted to define it
as being faithful to what you really are. Let's talk
about that, what you are: turned earth, sticky pith,
bitter milk of dandelion stems. Admit it. In this creation
no matter what gets sowed you'll always be *slut*,
never *gardener*. Who wouldn't ache for something new?
You keep busy, count all the beasts, catalogue
every flying, crawling, swimming, wriggling, curled-up,
unfurling you can find. You've got books, big ideas.
But you're forever cleaning up somebody else's feathers
and wax. Leaning on a broom, giving in to nostalgia
as robins burble their evening song, you watch a boy
aim for the net, over and over. You almost feel the ball
leave his hands, each near miss trailing a helix
of disappointment and aspiration. Awkwardness
punctuated by grace. A boy becoming what he is. Making
what he can make. Practicing. You made him that way.

The Mothers

We're a plowed field, furrow after furrow
open to glowering sky.
We have no reserve, gravity

and physics work against us, we're spilling

out of our best strapless dress,
its pattern of tulips alternating with something—
ribbon, house, bluebird—

undecipherable, blurred

like yesterday's newspaper
put down to catch the mess of seed and flesh
we hollowed out

for three grinning faces.
We used our bare hands. We're without

shame. We're good and determined

to get at that sweet spot, and if we don't actually
love when their kisses leave wet
on our cheeks

and if, periodically, we let the sun go down

on our resolve, if our dress
shows wear, the hem's perfect ellipse
revealing a sad droop,

that's just a blip, an aberration, a bit of fodder
for stories passed around the fire

washed down with our meat and milk.

We're bigger than that. We're all in.
We've put the garden to bed, banked
the foundation, left one tap dripping

against the inevitable freeze,

and look how the sun shows itself
again, every day, between the trees.

You just have to get up,
pull back the heavy curtain
with the vine stitched into its length

and there it is: the world and its anvil.

On Sundays They Shoot at Nothing

And I am planting flowers.
The new year is coming.
And the shooters return every Sunday, designated hours, dawn to dusk.
Thick fog and I can almost imagine I'm somewhere else.
Each shot reverberates.
My old dog raises his head, deaf, but he feels it.
My husband is in year two of a diagnosis.
The shooting range is pretty, with picnic tables beneath a rustic shelter.
I've never seen anyone eating there.
No one knows how long it will take my husband to die.
Each person is different.
I don't know what they shoot at.
Silhouettes of torsos, cardboard cut-outs, concentric circles.
The weather has been unpredictable.
Supply chain disruptions continue, but still we have food on the shelves.
I did buy extra. In case. I did think about getting a gun.
No one I know has died recently from the virus.
And I'm boosted.
In the last school shooting students escaped through a window.
They filmed it. I didn't want to watch but I did.
I cry in the car when I'm driving.
A friend calls it titering my grief.
Like letting air out of a balloon, a little at a time.
Spellcheck wants to make it *tittering*. Almost the opposite.
Almost the same. Laughing just a little bit.

We Make Meaning by Doing (or Make Do by Meaning)

Meaning it's not enough for the cherry tree to stun
with blossom, but we must weight its branches, make them kneel
and weep. Some gardeners are famous for turning beauty
on its axis, raking pine needles not off the path
but on, while others haul out their motors and blow
whatever's in the way out of the way. We want messy gone,
like how I sometimes ache to switch off my son's strobing
intensity, unwind my daughter from her gauzy shroud
of what appears to be disappointment occasionally pierced
by sunlight. Or maybe it's my husband's brain I'd like to overhaul,
give a good Roto-Rooter to those mysterious crevasses
into which patience, with her weak ankles and limp handkerchief
SOS, seems to have disappeared. Help certainly is not on the way.
And what do you make of that? I ask myself, knowing
the answer I'm chasing will break my hull in two, swallow me
whole, meaning: *I'd rather not say* and *everything.*

My Friend Says "Meant" Instead of "Supposed"

As in, *it's meant to get cold this week.* Doesn't it
feel better that way? Like somebody's in charge.
The way the deer that darted in front of my car
meant to outrun my bumper, put centuries
of DNA behind that intention. It worked.
We're both OK. We took a breath and jumped
to a different page in the story. I'm not sure
about the deer, but I got to admire the reservoir,
now they've taken down the trees along the road
and we're meant to see beauty we could only
suppose was there before: low winter sun
on water glittering like the scales of an enormous
fish, little fishes swimming in its belly. That fractal
logic. It occurs to me that these are pieces
of a very large puzzle. My dendrites yearn
toward a solution—they're hard-working
little stars—but even they can't wrap their bright
tentacles around it, there's only so much
we can process: blur of deer, disappeared trees,
the wind-borne acorn that smacked my windshield
so hard it made me jump. It occurs to me
that had I been on foot, that acorn might've
drilled into my brain like a rogue meteor. But I'm
guessing that's not how I'm meant to go.
When I lie awake at night, scanning constellations
behind my eyes, that's not what I suppose.

No Birds Were Harmed in the Making of this Poem

Language is fossil poetry, Emerson said, in reference to
I know not what, possibly
an aster in stony clay, a theory of light.

Something that finds its way out.

And yes, that's me with the backhoe, digging.
That's me ripping out stitches, making and remaking, going
too far with the scissors.

Me with the bulging bag of scraps.

(My mother always said you can never have
too many good, clean rags.)

Speaking of my mother,
she wanted me to find someplace else to be young.
Why don't you do something productive? She'd mutter

as I stumbled from bed to couch
to towel on the lawn, slippery with baby oil,
not even reading a book.

Back then we didn't know what the sun could do to you.

Didn't know our emissions
were breaking down the membrane between us
and the atmosphere, what we used to call *outer space*.

Speaking of breaking,

today I almost ran over two ducks and a rooster
wandering around in what they mistook for freedom.

They were trying to expand their horizons
but I was so busy in my head, so far down the list of projects
I've abandoned, I didn't notice.

Though once past the fowl by sheer luck I didn't kill,

I snapped to for an orange sign that said *BUMP*,
and woke to a sudden preponderance of hydrangeas, yards
bustling with pale rockets of lacey bloom.

I set them aside for later

with the man who almost sold one to me
until I decided I couldn't trust him and testily abandoned the plants
in the little red wagon I'd been pulling around.

I gave up on that project before I'd even left the nursery,

and was chewing on something entirely different
when I flew by the very blonde girl in her driveway
swinging a jump rope

so that the business end was flying dangerously close
to somebody's cherry Camaro.

Boy, did she look happy about it.
She looked me dead on, her whatever it was–intention, will, mission–
her creative project

beaming right through the windshield of my car.

Thank you, little blonde girl for unsuspending my belief. I hope
you don't mind being stolen.

Ultramarine

> "This woman's story could have remained hidden forever…
> It makes me wonder how many other artists we might find in
> medieval cemeteries—if we only look."
> —Christina Warinner, University of Zürich

I offer you this: jawbone of a medieval woman
with a nugget of lapis lazuli embedded in her teeth. Blue

planet in the firmament of her calcified plaque.
She licked her paintbrush. Tongued vermillion, ochre,

iron gall. Blue above all. Virgin blue. I have tasted
that mineral tang, worshipped the feel of those sable hairs

coming to a point in my mouth. And I have tasted
disappointment. Overreaching. Hubris. Too many trips

to the water jar, too heavy a hand, boring into each bright
circle until my beautiful idea dissolves into a colorless

puddle. Like history, reflecting only the brightest sun, whitest
clouds. History, shallow and opaque. But this woman.

Maybe she escaped marriage, duty, sex. Maybe she was
devout. Either way, I see her at work, a few rare

pigments lined up in ceramic jars, parchment crowded
with someone else's calligraphic text, Book of Days,

a treatise on the sin of ambition or pride, lust or desire,
or instructions for divining a true virgin: *Upon fumigation*

with dock flowers, if she is a virgin she immediately
becomes pale, and if not her humor falls on the fire

and other things are said about her. Other things said
inside our very own mouths. Other falls and fires.

Poem Moonlighting as Tether

I lie in bed, hands stacked like wood
on my chest. I don't know if I'm trying
to start a fire, keep warm, disappear
like a rabbit in a thicket, or simply
add ballast to tether my body, keep
from spinning out. I press against
my caged breath, darkness inside straining
to meet dark outside, crossed arms
like dead Ophelia drifting downstream,
minus flowers, water, ode, just my wrists'
faint pulse contrapuntal to faint heart
thump. Hands like empty pockets.
Hands like vacant cradles. Lullaby
to no one. I get up, weak kneed, lungs
slowly deflating balloons, stare
at the sky clotted with stars oblivious,
insultingly bright, seemingly so close
you could pull them down. But not. Yes,
I know what they say we're made of.

Through Line

Innumerable robins, dandelions
gone over to perfect

overexposures poised for release an iron bridge
spanning a steep-sided river, shadows

falling sideways through the cables:
no climbing, no jumping, no rappelling

at any time   the roadside
an uninterrupted stream of ripening

timothy, bird noise and cow
their brown and white arrangement, their undisguised

inquiry as we pass   breaking up space
like the barbed wire's staccato

of uprights and horizontals   a flimsy boundary
when you consider

what we're made of   and that somebody
—despite the brand new barn's

acknowledged comforts and the farmer
checking for gaps

hawkweed, celandine and buttercup
might mask—

somebody   might change their mind
something   could break

and how would we know with all of this
blooming   this temporary

rise and fall and light rain softening our edges?

Getting Rid of the God's Eye My Child Made

Except it looks more like the eye of Sauron
or the snake in God's garden than any eye
I imagine a god would have. If I ever imagined
that, which I don't, because if I think of God
it's as photosynthesis, fractals, migration,
light on water. And my daughter is no longer
my daughter, because she's chosen *they*, or was
chosen, made that way, and they are fluid,
the way my god is fluid, one thing slipping
gently into the next, one element making room
for another, the way it's hard to say exactly
when it stops being night, or if teal is blue
or green. And the eye they made when they
was she is a halfhearted effort at obedience:
sticks and faded yarn arranged in concentric,
vaguely rhomboid shapes, some camp craft
to prove to parents progress is made. This ersatz
eye hung from a nail on the porch so long
it became invisible, the way things do when we
see them every day. Until today, when I took it
down, tossed it onto the kindling pile. They
and I will make a fire, we will warm ourselves.

It's Arguable

—for D.D.

These last weeks, I continue
filling the feeder, accidently-on-purpose
dropping a little seed on the ground
for the mice, whom I can't help loving
in the abstract, but whose traps remain
baited. There are limits
not only to my kindness, but my
imagination, huddled inside its silk and wool,
chewing on a bit of Bachelard
my teacher liked to quote: "I am caught up
in the perplexing dialectics…of the infinitely
diminished." She found the only high enough
place in the neighborhood
from which to jump. She was determined
and then she was diminished. Left
to imagine what she saw
on the way down I can only conjecture
it had something to do with a net
more open than closed.

II

Unbecoming

Why do they call it a slight when it's really a slice, a sky
shot through with August lightning troubled by glowering

cirrus? Lowered, low-pressure clouds, brows, the glare that begat
your corresponding squint. Your ache. You can't keep telling

that story. Everyone's shifting in their seats, desperate
for the exit. And you say *fuck* too much. It's unbecoming,

doesn't become anything. Unlike the actual act of unprotected
procreation no seed gets planted, becomes bloom. No begatting

ensues. Therefore, learn to ignore. To abhor. Rhyme
when nothing else will do. Know that sound is a barrier

you punch through. On the other side is what? That cave
where the first people painted their dreams? We called them

something. We made them nothing. Begat them out of history.
White-washed their walls. We can do that from here. Steal dreams

when we can't find ours. What's left is a box of toy soldiers,
like the ones my friend methodically cut the guns from,

so her son wouldn't know people shoot people. Wouldn't want
to shoot. It didn't work. He made a gun from his finger,

scrap of wood, half-eaten buttered toast. He begat his way
to death in the abstract, all those plastic men holding nothing

in their arms. Pointing to the horizon where a white whale
breaches and spumes. Another blowhard story of obsession

and possession, tit begatting tat. *I'm rubber you're glue.*
Got you back. Got your back. I want you back. Which leads us

to singing. Because we've got to use our mouths for something.
Kissing, if possible, whistling, if not, which keeps us safe

in the dark. (They say.) (From well-lit rooms.) Calls the faithful
dog back to us. The one who stole the bone, buried your heart.

O the heart, you knew you'd end up here. Fuck. *Sing something.*

Because the Moon is a Cliché & Not Exactly Steadfast

Moon, hearts, stars, flowers.

All of the above. And by above I mean where the stars are pinned, winking
as they burn.

Because I'm not allowed to talk to the moon anymore.

Because the moon has amnesia. A sideways smile that becomes a blind eye.
The moon is a recurring mistake, history's dumb rotation.

If you're going to touch me that way, I want you to look at me.

If you're going to touch me. Which we've agreed will never happen.

But let's say I could address you. Let's say a rag-rich page lay before me, blank,
white as your deckled skin, and I'm the one in the morning coat,
a velvet collar for my chin to brush against, consumptive quill in my grip,
blood spot on my handkerchief.

What would I say to your vacant expanse? Something like, *Moon, this time,
take me with you when you go. Or, Moon, are you really that cold?*

Isn't heartache sweet? It tastes of everything you ever wanted. The rain-soaked
lilacs I pressed my face into as a child, knowing, even then, something I needed
was there, unreachable.

If you're going to touch me, I want you to drink the water from those lilacs.

Crickets

Why did they choose them to signify silence? I can't
think of anything louder announcing the end. Come
high, hot July, our green sphere tilting
toward arid fall, males fiddle their wings intensely,
advertising availability, seeking fertility
with a song potential mates hear below the knees.
So much vibration. A song for sex, afterglow,
a song even to make the females fight. Courtship
mirroring our own, but loud, with none of the pretense
humans have crafted, our under-the-radar
mute language of love, or what passes for love.
Emotional sleight-of-hand. Accidental contact.
Warm breath in your ear. You can tell how hot it is
by how loud the crickets sing. *Some things
are best left unsaid*, you say, and play and play.

Another Message from the Body

We want to be autonomous, we want to go
back to sleep, back to the dream

where somebody's petting us like a cat.
We've elected our own government, it is us.

We're unified, we have currency, and we demand
more pleasure, less time off. We want exercise,

especially swimming, we like that weightless feeling
but we think the ocean overrated. We've had it

with salt. Also, we strongly suggest a more subtle
tongue and don't understand why it's so hard

to find comfortable, good-looking underwear.
Speaking of which, we humbly request fewer hours

in our clothes. Did we already say that?
By the way, we enjoy how you settle your hand

just at the oarlock of our hip. It makes us feel
a little nautical, as if we're being steered

but in the very best way, like you're making sure
we don't miss the albatross that's taken flight.

Another Lesson in Failure and Desire, or Leonardo's To-Do List

I thought I was through. Not with the body. With uncertainty.
What does this have to do with desire? Everything.

Look at Leonardo's to-do list:
*1. Talk to Giannino, the Bombardier, re. the means by which the tower
of Ferrara is walled without loopholes.*
2. Ask Benedetto Potinari by what means they go on ice in Flanders.
3. Draw Milan.

Look at my list:
1. Figure out if you can cheat without calling it cheating.
2. Find a way to pleasure that doesn't hurt (anyone.)
3. Map a route back to yourself before you were broken.

At first glance it may appear ambitious. (I may have to settle
for a process of elimination, a system of wanting.)

*4. Ask about the measurement of the sun promised me by Maestro
Giovanni Francese.*

4. Find a way to measure the circumference of of how you wake up:
by what increments and at what angle does light penetrate
the blinds? As you turn your back on morning, what do you turn
into?

(Not sleep. Possibly a dream, a manufactured promise, some kind of
highly personal extortion.)

*5. Find a master of hydraulics and get him to tell you how to repair
a lock, canal and mill in the Lombard manner.*

(Apply pressure, breathe. Apply pressure. Build a boat.)

Enough with the boat, you don't even like being at sea. You've never handled a sextant, can't name a constellation.

5. Find your loophole, crack in the wall, means to traverse thin ice.

It's possible I'm a liar. I have nothing with which to refute that accusation, other than my skin, with its thousands upon thousands of nerve endings rippling like wheat in unsettled weather.

6. *Get the master of arithmetic to show you how to square a triangle.*
7. *Get Messer Fazio to show you about proportion.*

(Leonardo imagined what he couldn't see or know. Distractible, curious, he didn't always finish what he started.)

A knowledge of the inner workings of the body are key.

6. In our minds it was beautiful, it all worked.

I Carry Myself

like the stars I'm supposed to be made of

are collapsing. Or I've swallowed them, constellated
my very own black hole. And what's wrong

with darkness? It's there we conceive, where our cells
do their math, multiplying into you and me. I want more
than I am. Is it that simple? I'm never enough, though

according to the celestial maps I am two. Divided.
Undecided. And I want more than my fair share
of sky. My mother used to say my eyes were bigger
than my stomach. She was right. I saw too much.

Couldn't keep it down. Does that mean we saw the same?
A dark question. Unanswerable, as she's long in the earth,
mouth and eyes sewn shut. (Sorry you had to see that.)

I tried, I tried, to make her see. Asked for nothing. Hoping
she'd kiss me with a mouth unfull of no. Not ever.

I have ideas about love. They're broken right here.

Broken/Bent

You say *broken*, I say *bent*. Coaxable. Coax me
into candescent. From bulb to bloom, from bruised
white to *wine-dark*. If the sun ever breaks through
these ice-sodden clouds I might feel rescued, coaxed.
If the sun ever breaks through. Tonight, they're calling
for shooting stars. We call them that even though
they're neither, just scraps of dust and rock burning
in Earth's atmosphere. Yesterday I remembered again
my brother is dead. His death not a hoax. He's not
coming back, even if we coax him with Vicodin,
vodka, marshmallow Fluff. He liked to burn. He was
never really my brother so I have to remind myself
he's gone. Or because he was, I have to forget.

Ideas

I've run out of ideas but keep going,
even though many of us are quitting, leaving
for the first time in droves. Drove, as in drover
or driven, as in cattle, herded by a few guys
on horses. What drives beasts to be driven?
We buy into things. Ideas about ourselves.
I'm good at this, not that. We box ourselves
in, drag the heavy gate behind us, stare longingly
out at the plains. I was a good student until
I wasn't. Didn't apply myself. After a point.
After geometry, when we got to equations
where X stands in for something else. I couldn't
get X. But I liked our handsome teacher
so effort forthcame. X marks the spot where
I began to innocently lust. Yearn. Whatever
you want to call it, so it doesn't sound dirty.
At that age yearning was potent but abstract.
I wanted someone to shine light on me,
to be X. I wanted out of the pack, to howl.
But I knew where the fences were. I licked salt
from the rails, swished my tail, ruminated.

Of Them All

I ruin everything in me. I mean everything
I'm *in*. I'm mean to what's *mine*,
even though I *made* them. *Sad*, I mean,
I made them *sadness* instead of *cupcakes*
or *consolation* or even *a good hot bath*
and now the not-sweet's *cooked*, the mirror's
all *spit-shine* and *glare,* I fucked with its
luster, it's stuck to me, stuck to the stories
I keep telling myself, fairy tales minus
wolf, *stepmother*, *witch*,
just the woodcutter and his wife,
chop, chop, chopping away
while the children hoard their *crumbs*.
They're lost to the woods, me to the trade
I took for something *solid*. I *meant*
too much. Thought I made me a *deal*.
Proud owner of a flowerless stem. Clouds
you can't see into. This home sweet climb.

Because the World Has Its Own Version of Solace

in a field of decapitated corn stalks
on the corner of Reed's Bridge and Elm
a flock of wild turkeys scratched
as if something nourishing remained
between the rows of dry stubble, interrupting
a disappointment I can't now remember
but at that moment rose in my body
like fever-driven mercury
from those perilous, pre-digital years
when I once spent an undocumented hour
with the unprotected tip of my finger,
playing with quicksilver spilled
from a thermometer I dropped.
I was taken by the element's reluctance
to break, its talent for self-repair, reshuffling
molecules around a breach to form again
a perfect, otherworldly bubble,
when all I could be was the same
girl sealed inside the held
breath of what might come, watching
for some as yet unnamed law of attraction
to upend and shake me, hard, until something
resembling danger, but soft,
came loose and made me
disappear and different and away.

Liminal

An eagle announces itself. You look up,
try to catch the sun glancing off
the white of its head, so you can be sure.
You hate to call something what it's not.
A fox pauses mid-stride, locks eyes,
keeps going. Flaming bottle brush tail
an unspoken insult to your hairless
vulnerability. You're just a memory.
A scent. A rabbit zigzags, freezes, tries
to look like anything other than helpless.
You're the rabbit, silent and frozen.
You type your name into another SOS text,
and it autocorrects to *Any*. That this feels
significant is significant. You'll take any sign
you can get. That you hold this mirror
up to your distorted image gets you points,
no clarity. Bravery of sorts. That you seek
to make something from what's disappearing,
falling away, ending makes you what?
Any. Any port in a storm. Any day now.
Any chance of a cure. Anyone.

Rabbits

What I came to say is lost, half-hidden,
stilled in the shade of a beach rose,
like the fat rabbits here

at land's end, soft inner elbow
of sand & bay

where the pale, retired bank examiner
who *pretty much owns everything around here*
accuses a woman of trespassing;

I don't need this today,

she spits through tears, attempts to leave,
but her dog's caught rabbit scent,

& it becomes a leashed tug of war
we're not supposed to watch.

The patriarch's loose-limbed son & ginger-haired,
carbon copy grandsons
break the tension running after their kite

hung up in the bushes where another rabbit's
hunkered down, waiting

for us to leave. The woman finally drags her dog away.

We wait for a break in the clouds.

My husband, newly disabled, hobbles to the shoreline,
wades in, floats, for some moments
weightless, grateful,

then struggles up the slight incline, a few yards
that shift and trip him up. People stare.

He's not beautiful
like he was.

A woman smiles, congratulates me
on getting my "father" in the water.
I smile back, feel the shock of it

later, like a sunburn

& when I'm alone with the deep blue hydrangeas
nodding their heavy heads in agreement,

touch the spot on the back of my head
where my hair isn't, a dime-sized absence.

Stress, my hairdresser says, and I make a joke.

Coming in with the tide: detritus, sulfurous
kelp stink, unanchored floats, plastic.

I'm mostly treading water, but I'll have to
come in, too: the ocean loves no one & everyone
will soon see the long sand bar, grief

laid bare, all the places
the ordinary, plain & dear appear & disappear.

III

Fixed/Blue/Gone

When the house began to empty
it was almost spring.

Beneath the leafless oak, blue
squill pushed through

patches of snow, surrounded
an empty pizza box

guarding the lawn
like a tied-out, barking dog.

For a while, she was fixing
up the place: little statues, a blue

wading pool for the kids.
There was a car, she got them to school

pretty much on time.
Then that was gone, too,

and some nights red, white and blue
cruiser lights washed up against the house.

You knew they were fighting.
You could hear it, you could

practically see through gaps in the siding
they never managed to fix, imagine

in winter, heat from the fire
rushing back out, somebody's fingers

possibly blue with cold.
March, no smoke in the chimney,

just an empty, pounded down spot

and frayed blue tarp

where cordwood used to be.
Then she was in jail, and all around

the house tall grass, blown
lilacs, wild rose swallowing

junked lawnmowers and tractors
he used to fix for a little cash,

along with the weed he sold
he said, to keep himself in smoke.

April, I gave him and the oldest boy
a ride, both of them twitching,

sweating in the back seat—
his boy and my girl the same age—

and I made small talk.
High summer and the house gone

dark, cardboard for windows,
wheelbarrow heaped with dirt, shovel

set against it, like someone thought
they were coming right back.

I Want to Rearrange the Furniture Around a Fire

but we have no fire,
only ice coming down from the sky as one thing,
hitting the ground as something else.

I don't speak that language,
so I listen, wait

for somebody or something to blink.

Until then, no remedy
but extra layers, uncurtained windows,

a bit of harmless peeping
as the day comes to its end
and the merchants shutter their shops.

I want to applaud

the backlit silhouette of a barber
setting his implements to rights.

Such an intimate performance.
Such a small theater.

And when the café parks a dirty bucket
and mop in the middle of the floor
I know what it means:

We're closing, don't ask for anything.
But I do, because I have to.

Sitting by the window eating soup
I could become the symbol for what
from the sidewalk looks like comfort,
but I never imagined myself

as hearth. The chair and footstool, the children
who want me to share. I didn't believe

I could strike that spark, ignite.

Or I could, but it was a slow burn
and so much ash to sift through.

Everywhere is by a door
and every door keeps opening. Cold
air rushes in. From outside,

the rooms where other people live

are deep yellow, like a daffodil
a few days after it's picked. Maybe

that's what I want. The glow,
and the distance. The possibility
I might enter.

Casting Off

Requirements: cast bread on water. Crumbs.
Tiny fishes eat the crumbs, dead skin from your heels and toes.
Heart-shaped stones on the rocky bank. Not many, but a few.
Resentments: not many, but persistent, lingering, damaging.
Why not just finish it? Feel it first. Then wave goodbye.
Like a child, hand opening and closing. Little starfish, octopus.
Because you need help. *Not waving but drowning.*
Coming full circle, wheel of the year, traditions, habits, ritual.
Relationships: let them go, your tender child selves, wading in.
Brush the table off, your lap. You haven't moved.
You don't have to rescue them. The crumbs. The children.

True Nature/Boneless

True Nature?, the note on my laptop asked.
My son, who finds whatever I hide,

crossed it out, wrote, *Boneless.* It's his joke
of the moment, all-purpose answer. I followed

his lead, camouflaged my flesh with flowers,
an anchor, a heart shot through with a dagger,

emblazoned with *Mom.* But my skeleton
persisted, pointed to the latest hole I was digging.

So many holes for so many daffodils, so much
tender hope for spring: yellow trumpets,

powdery stamens and reproductive organs
that look exactly like what they are. Hollow

stems like the bones of a bird. Did I say
I was on my knees? The ground almost frozen,

and the wind bending everything down?
That's the kind of faith I need. To still be

here, when those green knives break ground.
Even when I write *her* instead of *here.*

Knit/Unravel

I went looking for snowdrops. Wanted proof, even in this winter
of limp dregs— yellowed circulars for stores no one visits, clothes
with zippers quiet in the closet, all of us dragging our bodies around
through dirty snow—that something new would come the way it's
always come: shrill chorus of spring peepers, redwing blackbirds'
brash call.

No snowdrops, but the pale stem of one intrepid daylily pushing up
through hoarfrost, oak leaves, empties and plastic nips. Someone on
this road needs to hide the evidence. Someone on this road might not
want to go home.

No snowdrops, but sap buckets on maples, slow drip, fast boil. I sit
in the same chair, knit and unknit a hat the color of mint. Sometimes
I wonder who figured it all out—who thought to tap and evaporate
the colorless almost nothing running through trees into something
sweet? Who saw sheep and thought, sweaters? Who decided to pray?
Where does patience come from?

No snowdrops, not yet. I walk the loop. Knit, unravel, wind yarn
back on the ball.

Forecasting

November thieves light. Its groaning,
overstuffed table force feeding

December's mandatory twinkle. Sticky
sugar & shine. A buffer for the hangover

January brings, when we huddle & low, hay damp
in our shuttered mangers, pockets emptied

of savings & saviors, just as February's crash
blows in a day late & short. Not even pretending

to believe in renewal, we shuffle into March,
Googling *chilblains, ides, suspicious moles* & despite

its reputation for cruelty & well-advertised cheat,
take April into our arms. We'd fuck it

if we could. Invite anything pink to our beds
that comes fast and sings of mud & May

breaking winter whites into green & yellow
throats opening to warm June rain. Now

amnesiacs, light-drunk solstice revenants,
moon children & flower children & wide-eyed

July fireworks worshippers, we don't hear
reports as cannons, but waves. We're oiled up,

salty August, buoyant, summer forever,
until September's sere nudge, stark V of geese

overhead, frogs exiting stage right, (yes,
pursued by a bear) taking green, leaving orange,

then red & brown & October's grin
& wink & beauty & wind & hollow.

Flowers That Bloom Early & Disappear
They Call Ephemeral

Witch hazel unfurls its ragged, yolk-yellow stars,

     and herons arrive, awkward bodies

hunched astride their haphazard nests

     empty and silent for now, but soon—

and robins return puffed up, strutting,

     to yank at whatever dares emerge from the dirt,

and the light is back, inching up the horizon,

     at close of day a different slant,

and the shadblow buds bloom as the actual shad spawn

     in the river, and everywhere water,

rushing down hillsides, filling ponds

     where frogs crawl out of the cold mud

to racket their flag of availability, family,

     and mate, even after months frozen they've not

abandoned desire, and I feel it too, in my body

     and the body of the world, how inside us

a kind of clockworks uncoils, loosens,

     unticks our minutes, makes space, as if to say,

I'm here, it's safe, you can open, it's safe, open.

To the Editor Who Said He Doesn't Publish Nature Poems

If you heard a sigh of relief it was me. Neither tree—
bare or leafed—nor bird—winged or warbling—

gets past my poesy. Ditto for posies. Nothing smells
as sweet as anything, my love is like a red, red

zero, and certainly nothing art sick. No creature's
examined once—much less 13 times—and therefore

we're safe from all that lumber, gambol, whinny,
mew or trumpet. Expect nary a reference to water,

likewise earth, wind or fire, unless it's one of my
favorite 70's bands and then, I italicize. It's ironic.

And I am not wandering lonely in the pastoral, I refuse
to arise and go now unless I'm actually ready to go now

and please, nothing of clay-and-wattles made, (whatever
wattles are) no hills, distant or dark, shrouded in mist,

tattooed with cirrus, forget blood-orange sunsets,
chiaroscuro, beauty—please, no beauty! terrible

or otherwise, no wonder, curiosity, nothing of this
world that's solidly before us, nothing about which,

if I were that kind of poet, I would find words.

Unmet

Hard edge of the road blurred
by fallen leaves, yellowed

needles, drifts and layers,
cracked asphalt, this body

a dog that won't stay home.
You a mulberry bush

(round and round we go).
This body a map, longitudes

and lassitudes, this whole body
an unstrung harp, lost notes.

Thus begins the weather
unsettled, heart as gate

banging on its latch, heart
as towel thrown in,

heart as 3am. Self-portrait
as peeling wallpaper.

Self-portrait as unthreaded eye.
Self-portrait as beehive,

as buzzing, the promise of sweet
unmet, impending sting.

Self Portrait As

starlings massed in a sycamore
their dark racket

their blur
Self portrait as low tide

confederate
of sand flea and riprap

and yes! sunshine
on water, refracted

as flickering, as view
from a train window

torn collage
of asphalt, graffiti, rags

somebody's bed for the night
Self-portrait as woe

haste and packing tape
jimmied lock

shaky-legged kids
no one's hand to hold

Self-portrait as girl
leaning into a single shaft of light

(she might be reading a letter)
as black marks on a page

as scumble, crazing, foxing, impasto
a twice-mended cup

Self-portrait as raised voice
risen bread, cold coffee

your reflection in a highly polished spoon
horse ridden round and round in its ring

Maybe This Poem Isn't About the Soul

but it could be about distraction, static,
white noise salting the air. Open your mouth
and catch it on your tongue. It might taste
sad, like yearning, white sails coming home
or leaving again. You might need to say
if you're on board, declare colors, finally
undertake that tutorial on knots. Up, over,
around and through. Square, slip, noose.
You could start with that frayed rope
trailing its insignificant wake. Not the soul,
but ripples. Not distraction, doubt. You could
stand up in the boat. Try out your legs.
That is, if you're feeling something you can't
put a finger on: high summer's December
undercurrent numbing your ankles, soul
loose on its moorings: bump, drift, bump.

Bit Hard

Even the lilacs remind me of my transgressions,
how the tree I planted thrived and bloomed, stank
sweetly in its little spot beside my window.
How I yanked it out, then stood in the gaping hole,
weeping. Like that fairy tale girl who wants
nothing to eat but the bitter greens growing lush
in someone else's garden, I'm never satisfied.
Even here, snug in our world of violets and perfection,
there's a crack in the glass, a hair off. That rub.
If the girl were here now, I'd advise her
to observe the tulips, how they give themselves over
to gravity, I'd have her listen to the sound
the crow makes on its rusted hinge, I'd make her
notice the new baby goat in its warm rectangle
of sunlight. Isn't it enough? I'd ask her,
and go back to my digging, plant my spade deep.

Three Times Removed

You watch a kid make his halting way
down the sidewalk, and pity him

for his limp, but it turns out
he's only trying to avoid the cracks.

He's playing a game, and you,
as usual, are making shit up,

embroidering fancy French knots
onto a cloudless day, then picking

the stitches out, calling absence
space. As if you needed more

room for emptiness.

*   *   *

Why can't you just tell a story?
Why don't you have a story to tell?

Today you remembered your mother
at her end. You said aloud, *that still hurts.*

You thought about your friend,
how the only way she can bear her loss

is to make it rare. Then you kept driving,
the way she has to keep acting out

her life, try not to touch the vacancy.

*   *   *

Oak, dogwood, sycamore, brick,
two strips of orange light.

If you understood math, the geometry
of trees and sky might tell you

where you fit, prove *this, therefore, that.*
Instead, you distract yourself

with the balcony's wrought iron
flourishes, a little softcore

graffiti: a quick pink heart
someone's chalked on the wall, a *you,*

with the *hey* smudged out.

     *   *   *

Why don't you just say what it is?
Like that table on the curb

that says it's free. You're meant
to take it home, but you'd rather make it

into a joke: imagine the table
on its back, legs in the air, a capsized

beetle, dead cartoon dog.
Plato would say the table isn't free,

because everything we make
is a lie, because we aren't God,

with his endless revisions.

     *   *   *

So what if you make the best lie
you can? Right the table. Lay it

with china, platters groaning
with something stuffed with something

stuffed with something else. The meat
that used to be walking around. Don't think

about the atoms we're made of
and why we don't fall,

keep falling. The cracks.
Don't spoil it for yourself. Tell yourself,

I love this lie. It may not be
perfect, but it's mine. I never want this lie

to end. To leave the table, to be free.

Acknowledgements

With thanks to the editors of these publications, in which the following poems appear:

Adroit Journal: "Poem Moonlighting as Tether"

Alaska Quarterly Review: "Getting Rid of the God's Eye My Child Made," "Sweet"

AMP: "Another Lesson in Failure and Desire, or, Leonardo's To-Do List"

Barrow Street: "Bit Hard"

Beloit Poetry Journal: "Rabbits"

Connotations Press/Hoppenthaler's Congeries: "Another Message from the Body," "I Want to Rearrange the Furniture around a Fire"

Upstreet: "Of Them All"

Memorious: "Unmet"

Massachusetts Review: "Because the World Has Its Own Version of Solace"

Mom Egg Review: "I Carry Myself"

On the Sea Wall: "On Sundays They Shoot at Nothing,"

Orion: "Through Line"

Radar: "My Friend Says 'Meant' Instead of 'Supposed'"

Terrain.org: "Ambergris," "Knit/Unravel," "Liminal"

The Sun, "Forecasting", "Through Line"

Tin House: "Between"

Tuesday, an Art Project: "It's Arguable"

Waxwing: "Because the Moon is a Cliché & Not Exactly Steadfast,"

"Unbecoming" published as "No Begatting Ensues") "Wasp Nest,"
"(Eve) Talking to Herself (Mother's Day)"

Women's Review of Books: "The Mothers," "We Make Meaning by
Doing (or Make Do by Meaning)"

"Ultramarine" was awarded the 2022 Cecil Hemley Award from the
Poetry Society of America

"(Eve) Talking to Herself (Mother's Day)" is included in the anthol-
ogy, ***Between Paradise & Earth: Eve Poems***, Orison Books, Luke
Hankins, Nomi Stone, eds.

WBUR-Boston Public Radio and WFCR-New England Public Radio
aired and published on their web site, "Fixed, Blue, Gone" as part of a
segment on the opioid crisis in Massachusetts communities.

"No Birds Were Harmed in the Making of this Poem" appears on the
Massachusetts Cultural Council web site, ***Art Sake,*** for poetry fellows.

Notes

Ambergris, sometimes called "floating gold" is an extremely rare, solid, waxy, and flammable substance that originates from the digestive system of sperm whales. It's formed from the indigestible parts of the whale's diet, primarily the beaks of cuttlefish and squid, and is highly sought after as a fixative for perfume. From the Middle English *ambregris*, Middle French *ambre gris*, or yellow gray.

Ambergris: This poem was inspired by a story in the June 11, 2021, *Cape Cod Times* about a Cape Cod lobster diver who claims he was swallowed by a humpback whale and then spit back out into the water. *Cruciform, coronate,* and *campanulate* are all botanical terms used to describe specific shapes of flower corollas.

On Sundays They Shoot at Nothing: The first line of this poem comes from a cartoon by José María Nieto, in which one character asks another. "Why so optimistic about the new year? The other says, "I think it will bring flowers." "Yes? How come?," the other asks. "Because I am planting flowers," the other replies.

Another Lesson in Failure and Desire, or Leonardo's To-Do List: Lines in this poem are culled from a page in one of Leonardo DaVinci's notebooks, translated by Robert Krulwich.

Casting Off: Not waving but drowning is the title of a poem by Stevie Smith.

About the Author

Amy Dryansky's (she/her) first book, *How I Got Lost So Close to Home*, won the Kinereth Gensler Award from Alice James Books, the second, *Grass Whistle* (Salmon Poetry) received the Massachusetts Book Award. A former poet laureate of Northampton, MA, she's also received honors from the Poetry Society of America, MacDowell, Massachusetts Cultural Council and Bread Loaf Writers' Conference. Individual poems appear widely in journals, as well as several anthologies. Dryansky parents two children and occasionally teaches creative writing, most recently as the James Merrill Visiting Poet at Amherst College. She is currently developing community-based workshops for caregivers and grievers.

www.ingramcontent.com/pod-product-compliance
Lightning Source LLC
Chambersburg PA
CBHW041213150726
48006CB00016B/2231